The Flame and the CANDLE

AMELIA BISHOP
Author and Photographer

BROADMAN PRESS
Nashville, Tennessee

Library of Congress Cataloging-in-Publication Data

Bishop, Amelia.
  The flame and the candle.

  1. Meditations.   I. Title.
BV4832.2.B5 1987   242   87-8071
ISBN 0-8054-5033-5

Contents

 **Power**

**Remembering
Eula Mae Henderson**

1   The Flame

It may have looked like an ordinary day
    That day in Jerusalem
    When the Holy Spirit came down
But it wasn't
A promise matured in the womb of time
    And came forth a happening
They may have looked like ordinary people
    That roomful of believers
But they weren't
    The flame on their heads
    Became the flame in their hearts
    And thrust them into history.

The mystery which has been hidden from the past ages and generations; but has now been manifested . . . Christ in you, the hope of glory (Col. 1:26-27, NASB).

It was a warm spring day many years ago, and the windows of the elementary school were open. Outside, a faint breeze stirred in the cottonwood trees and an ancient trolley car clanged in the distance.

Inside, the geography lesson began. The teacher pulled down a map of the Middle East and began to indicate the different countries, using a wooden pointer. She paused on what was then Palestine, now Israel.

"This is the country where Jesus lived." She tapped the map, indicating Bethlehem. "And this is where He was born." The pointer moved up to Nazareth. "He grew up here. . . . " The pointer moved down again. "Here is Jerusalem, and up north is the Sea of Galilee. You've read about these places in your Bible." She stepped back and surveyed the country. "Now the borders of Palestine . . . " The lesson continued.

One of her listeners sat transfixed on the third row. An eleven-year-old girl stared at the map, her brown eyes wide with wonder. An overwhelming thought had exploded in her mind, blotting out the room around her and the voice of the teacher. Suddenly she understood that Jesus, whom her parents had told her about all her life, was not just a story in a book, not a fictitious character "who went about doing good." He was real. They had said so, but somehow the living truth had not permeated. Now she realized that He had been born just like other people; He had lived; and He had died right there in that place on the map.

He was real.

A feeling of tremendous joy burst inside her and enveloped her in its tingling flame. Jesus was real! She wanted to jump up right then and tell everyone around her. "It's not just a story! He's real! He's real!"

And He is.

For some, His advent is sudden and dramatic; for others, it is a gradual dawning until He is formed in their hearts. For some, the flame leaps suddenly; for others, it is a warmth, then a glow, and then a light as understanding dawns.

For one little girl, He stepped from that map of Palestine. For others he comes in different ways.

But He comes.

He is real; He lives.

2 "Where Do You Live?"

"Penny for your thoughts"
    My friend's comment startled me
"Come back, wherever you are," she added, smiling
    "And from the look on your face
    That may be a long journey!"
She was right
I had dipped far back into yesterday
    Warming up mementoes in my treasure chest
    By the glow of remembrance
Sometimes we live too much in the past
    Or in the future
Sometimes we do it across the board
    Our personal life
    Our workaday life
    Our spiritual life . . . perhaps?

> **Seek the Lord while you can find him. Call upon him now while he is near (Isa. 55:6, TLB).**

"Where do you live?"

Newcomers attending a town gathering or a church function are often asked this question as friendships begin to blossom.

And the question is easily answered, ordinarily.

"I live in Texas . . . " Or it may be Alabama, Minnesota, or even Hawaii or Alaska.

But the question can be one that goes far deeper, far

broader, than first appearances would indicate. "Where do you live?" may question where we reside physically. But "living" may also indicate where we spend our time in the realm of the Spirit.

"Where do you live . . . spiritually?" In the past? The present? The future? The question is a pertinent one for the Christian.

As you living too much in yesterday? Are you relying on the spiritual fuel left over from some past moment with the Lord? True, it was a mountaintop experience. Like Peter, you did not want to come down; but like Peter also, you had to. And now?

There is nothing wrong with remembering those high moments of other days. But closeness to the Lord must flow forward from that time and must be fused with to-day's fresh experience. It must be a continuous and continuing process, not simply the memory of something that happened and is now locked into a segment of time, growing fainter as distance dims its remembered glow. It must be a part of today, fresh, vital, and vitalizing.

Are you living in the future? Do you spend your time resolving that tomorrow you will rearrange your priorities, set aside a definite time for Bible study, prayer, meditation? And furthermore, are you promising yourself that you will start early in the morning and "practice His Presence" as you move through your personal marketplace . . . ?

Perhaps you will.

But probably you won't . . . unless suddenly you see the link that ties it all together: spiritual highs are validated only by the response that follows. Devotion must lead to decision, and decision to deed.

Decisions and deeds are actualized in that frame of time we call today. Otherwise, they are either a memory or a promise.

"Where do you live?"

3   **The Lord's Overflow**

Another Monday, and I'm drained hollow
  Echoing on the inside
  Running on sheer nerves
  Or is it sheared nerves?
The day started well
  Conferences, committee meetings
Then the clutter hit the clock
    The computer's down
    The brochure's the wrong color
    And I need to shop for supper
What happened to this morning's euphoria?
The "I can handle it" attitude?
  I can't . . . obviously!

Now glory be to God who by his mighty power at work within us is able to do far more than we would ever dare to ask (Eph. 3:20, TLB).

"Whatever you do, don't spend the principal, the money you have invested. Spend the interest and the money will always be there."

The financial advice given the older couple by the banker made good sense. Their income would be sharply reduced in a few months; interest from investments would become a vital factor.

"Another way to say it is this," the banker concluded. "Always operate out of the overflow."

Which overflow?

Obviously the banker meant financial, but there is a message here for the Christian also. The coin of the realm is service, energy expended to meet expanding needs. But which overflow are we talking about?

There is an overflow that comes from ourselves: the extra spurt of energy beyond our personal needs, the "pushing" to fulfill obligations, the "I have committed myself and I will do it" frame of mind. Dependability is commendable, but the "overflow" in these instances is limited in both quantity and quality.

There is the overflow that comes from the Lord, totally unlimited in both quantity and quality. Scripture bears this out. "My God will supply all your needs" (Phil. 4:19) means what it says: ALL your needs. That includes your need to help those who turn to you, seeking assistance.

But the cup must be filled by the Lord before it can overflow; the process must be done daily because evaporation is at work. Heat of the day, whether anger, frustration, or bitterness, works to speed up the process.

When we allow "inflow" to be blocked for whatever reason, then the cup cannot be filled, and certainly it cannot overflow. We try to compensate by filling it ourselves. By sheer willpower we may be able to get the job done, but in the process we drain ourselves, and we supply the suppliant with second best. Both the use of the cup and its contents are limited since they come from us. Neither can be multiplied. "What you see, you get!"

Not so if we are operating out of His overflow. The source is limitless. It flows freely, meeting not only those needs at hand, but also those we do not even recognize.

Operate out of the Lord's overflow. It makes a world of difference.

It also makes a difference in the world.

4  The Credit Line

"I need to talk about this," my young neighbor said
"I have a long way to go in Christian growth
*   A very long way*
I worked so hard on the Easter pageant
*   I knocked myself out*
*   My family ate TV dinners for days*
Then, later, no one even said 'Thank you.'
And to make matters worse
They put Mary's name as chairman
*   And she wasn't even there half the time*
I thought I did it for the Lord
But if I did, why am I resentful?
*   And . . . honestly . . . why am I hurt?"*

Whatsoever ye do, do all to the glory of God (1 Cor. 10:31, KJV).

The fire crackled to life in the spacious fireplace, casting a flickering glow on the hearth. My friend and I stared into the darting flames, and then our attention was caught by a playful kitten. Fascinated by a ball of yarn, and batting it this way and that, she had succeeded in entwining parts of it about her small furry self.

We watched, amused, and then my friend, a former actress, reached for the kitten to disentangle the yarn. "We do this to ourselves, don't we," she commented. "We get all tangled up. Then ultimately, hopefully, we learn." After a bit she added, "And have you ever noticed how nice it is not to be tied to the credit line?"

Surprised, I turned my thoughts to money matters. "The credit line? Are you talking about borrowing money?"

"No, I'm talking about just the opposite. The ability to give and expect nothing in return.

"As a young Christian," she continued, "I wanted very much to live the Christian life, not just talk about it. And so I threw myself into church work. I was active in Sunday School, Baptist Young Women, and all of it. I even took part in civic affairs at the same time. But after a while, something began to dawn on me. I noticed that others were not working as hard as I was, and I also noticed that sometimes the work was rather thankless."

"Thankless?"

She looked at me and nodded. "You see, I thought I was doing it for the Lord like the Bible says, but I also wanted folks to know I was the one doing it. The Bible talks about the joy of giving, but we really don't understand that until we realize that giving truly means a gift—not a loan, nor a purchase, nor an exchange. You give it to the Lord, and move on. The transaction is complete. There is no second act. You fade into the scenery, rather than standing in center stage waiting for the spotlight.

"And when you've done this a few times, a new level of understanding comes through. There is a true, deep joy in the act or the fact of giving, and expecting nothing. You walk away unfettered by expectations. You feel an exhilarating sense of freedom."

I listened, trying to absorb not only her words but the expression on her face. "Quiet joy" and "serenity" came to mind.

By this time the kitten, freed of its entanglements, had scampered away. But the message remained.

"Don't get tied up in the credit line."

 **Light**

5  "My Problem IS Problems!"

I awakened in the curtained dimness of the room
*   Daylight rimming the edges of the drapes*
And stretched lazily beneath the warm covers
*   Savoring the new day*
Then it hit me
*   Jarring me awake*
"What am I going to do about . . . ?"
*   I don't know*
Today it looms larger than yesterday
*   Or does it just seem so*
*   Because I keep holding it off*
*   And yet I keep looking at it?*

I will lift up my eyes to the mountains; From whence shall my help come? My help comes from the Lord (Ps. 121:1-2, NASB).

The sound of laughter greeted the minister of youth as he entered the fellowship hall, laden with a fresh supply of dips and chips.

"What gives?" he called out, putting down the sacks.

"I have just reached a great decision," a tall youth responded. "I have figured out that my problem . . . is problems!"

And so it is. Quite often. Our problem is problems.

We have heard "It's not what happens to you, but how

you handle it that counts." But are we remembering that "handle" is an active verb?

Sometimes we are guilty of trying to ignore a problem, to "play like it's not there." Or we may wallow in the mire of indecision, thrashing about, and finally deciding to "put it off one more day," thus lengthening the quagmire. Or we may rush in and act hastily, proclaiming "Let the chips fall where they may!"

What to do?

Jesus had a way of going straight to the heart of a matter. Exactly what is the problem? Pinpoint it.

And then, talk about it. No, not over the backyard fence or around the table at coffee break. Instead, start at the Top. Talk with the Lord, putting into words not only what the problem is, but also how you feel about it. Ask for His help.

Talk also to professionals, if need be, and if you feel led to do so. (Does the problem involve drugs, or alcohol, or a family situation that counseling would help?)

Then comes the time to reach a decision and act upon it. Interestingly enough, "to act" may mean the deliberate decision to do nothing for the moment, but to await a specific time or circumstance. "Delayed action" does not always refer to a time bomb.

Or, "to act" may mean to take action now, deliberately, prayerfully.

Throughout the whole process, look through the problem to the reality of God, just as you look through the mists to the ocean beyond. Your vision may be limited, but you know from experience it is there. This is not to ignore the enigma that lies before you. Rather, it is to recognize that the God who holds the oceans in His palm is far greater than any possible problem. Concentrate on Him, not on the difficulty.

"I know whom I have believed."

6 Time . . . and the Numbers Game

It can't be five o'clock already
  Where did the day go?
I haven't done nearly all I needed to
  Correspondence unanswered
  Calls not returned
  And clothes at the cleaners
What happens to my days
  My weeks . . . my months
  They almost evaporate
And what happens to me in the process?

> **There is an appointed time for everything. And there is a time for every event under heaven (Eccl. 3:1, NASB).**

"What I need is a 36-hour day," the tired executive exclaimed, running his hand through his hair. "Maybe I could cope. My days just seem to be gobbled up. Or maybe I'm the one gobbled!"

Whatever the menu, be it the hours or the individual, the picture is hurried. It needs redrawing.

What is it that eats up our time?

To evaluate, some have found it helpful to select several "normal" days, and write down all activities, together with the approximate time involved.

In the total process, remind yourself that time is a

commodity. It may be invested; it may be spent. The first bears dividends; the second vaporizes.

What follows, then, is the heart of the matter: How can we invest our time in productive activity?

We might try a numbers game: subtracting, substituting, and adding. For example . . .

Each of us has responsibilities: the home, the church, the community, often the office. In each instance, certain assignments "go with the territory."

True. But the territory needs to be re-examined.

The mother feeds the infant, but the child should feed himself. The office manager trains the new assistant, but the incoming worker should soon be able to work alone. To continue the beginning type of ministry represents a disservice to all involved. The "server" is wasting time; the "servee" is denied growth.

Christian ministry involves meeting needs, but these must be real and contemporary. They must not be the "shoulds" begun in days of obvious need, and now carried over into months of pampering.

An adjustment is called for. It may be to subtract. Or it may be to substitute a ministry more in keeping with the current relationship, the present-day need.

Or perhaps the time problem has to do with adding. Additional responsibilities are knocking at your door. You want to help. But if your schedule is full, what are you going to eliminate or minimize? And if you have time slots for new activities, at what entry level? If numbers are not assigned—sometimes called priorities—activities clog the passageway, all trying to get in at the same time. Which comes first?

That's for you and the Lord to decide. If you don't, the new additions will push each other around the calendar. And you'll get pushed from one day to the next.

Subtracting, substituting, adding . . . will these stretch our time?

Perhaps not, but we will be stretched.

7 "Practice Makes Perfect" . . . Oh?

"Remember, there is a difference"
  The counselor said
"Between what a person does, and what he is."
  I can see that
  We all blow off at times
    Spin away on a tangent
    An orphan action
But I see something else also
  The more we do something
  The more it becomes us
    For better, for worse
Where will we be when the weeks stack together
  Higher and higher in time's storehouse
  Far better, far worse?

> **Practice living by the Spirit and then by no means will you gratify the cravings of your lower nature (Gal. 5:16, Williams).**

"Practice makes perfect." . . . Oh?

Not necessarily. It depends on what you are practicing.

To learn the multiplication tables and recite them perfectly is one thing. Only memory is involved.

To play a "perfect" game of tennis would be something substantially different. The whole array of human resources would be called into play: memory, understanding, evaluation, decision, motor skills, temperament, physical condition. The result might not be perfection, but practice would have been a strong factor in raising the level of performance toward the "ultimate."

No one would deny that practice greatly improves a tennis player. It is essential, as records indicate.

It is also significant to notice that practice affects not only the player involved, but also those around him. The opponent across the net, or perhaps his own doubles partner, each and all are impacted by whether or not he has "done his homework."

In the Christian arena, practice is also a factor in striving toward the top. We can deliberately program ourselves to desirable patterns of thinking and behaving, and the more we do it (practice it) the more it becomes "us."

Unfortunately, the same principle is at work on the negative side. While we do not "program negatively," our undesirable behavior sometimes slips through the gate when fatigue or anger has loosened the lock. And the more we allow this to happen, the more it becomes "us," also.

In essence, we are shaped by those practices we give time to.

"Wait a minute," you say. "In all this discussion, you haven't made something clear. Do you mean 'practice' as in 'to practice a play,' to rehearse? Or do you mean 'practice' as in 'the practice of taking a nap,' something you do every day? One means to repeat something a series of times; the other refers to an established pattern of behavior. Which is it?"

Think a moment.

Look in the mirror. Look around you.

They have blended together.

Practice (to repeat) and practice (your behavior) have become one.

A part of you.

8  Seeing Is Believing . . . Or Is It?

Seeing is believing
   Or is it?
Sometimes what I "see" in people or events
May be the projection of my own feelings
   "Just what I expected to see"
I have the uncomfortable feeling
Of sometimes looking through a scrim
   Created by my patterns of thinking
   Lights here, shadows there
It creates illusions on the stage
   Maybe it does in me too.

Since you have eyes can you not see with them? (Mark 8:18, Williams).

"I see what you mean."

"If he doesn't see your side of it . . ."

"Before you can reach a decision, you must see all the circumstances involved."

Often we use the word "see" when we mean "understand."

But the two are not synonymous. We do not always have "eyes that see" comprehending in truth the view before us. In part, this may be because "understanding" depends on "standing"—the place where you are.

In my town, "If you stand on the outskirts, you can see forever." But travel north less than a hundred miles, wind down a narrow road, and you will find yourself at the bottom of a red-walled canyon, your visibility limited to less than a quarter of a mile, in some places.

What you see depends on where you stand.

We may be too far off from a situation to see accurately. That is more easily handled. More often, we are too close.

How needful it is in times of dilemma for us to find a high plateau or mountaintop and enlarge our vision. All too often we have a keyhole concept. We see one side very clearly. Our close-up view may even illuminate the details, but only from one side. And that side is limited also because the surrounding areas which make up the total picture are blocked by the size of the keyhole.

We need to step back and step up.

Then, with the larger picture in perspective, we need to close our eyes and pray for clear eyesight, for vision undistorted by the patterns of previous thinking and feeling.

We can learn from history, but we are not locked into its concepts. If we learn, it is because we have used experiences as building blocks to new levels of understanding. Then, having reached higher ground, how foolish it is to reach back and pick up the lorgnette we used yesterday.

Today is in every sense a new day. It deserves a "fresh set of eyes" willing to see what is actually there. We must not superimpose what may have been there yesterday, nor what we thought was there the day before.

I will learn from the past, but I will not be limited by it. I will try to see today as it truly, truly is.

Some vistas may indeed look the same.

But some will be different.

Let me see them as they are.

As they are today.

Guidance

9  **Follow the Leader**

For weeks I had wondered
*   Should I go this way*
*   Or that*
Then something happened
*   Yesterday*
With a clarity of a vision I had my answer
That was yesterday
*   This is today*
I still have my answer
*   I still see my goal*
But it's there, and I'm here
And I don't know how to get there
*   It's dark outside.*

> **And the Lord will continually guide you,**
> **And satisfy your desire**
> **And give strength (Isa. 58:11, NASB).**

And suddenly, it was night.

We had been visiting, my friend and I, in the mountain cabin of a neighbor down the hillside. We had lingered too long. Stepping outside her front door to begin our homeward trek, I was startled by the abruptness of nightfall and the dense blackness of the night.

"Let's wait a minute," I said to my friend, "until my eyes get accustomed to the darkness."

"We can wait if you like," she replied. "But I don't

think it will make much difference. The moon's not up, and it's too hazy for starlight."

Beyond the pale circle cast by the porch light was a well of black, silent and forbidding. I stepped to the edge of the circle and hesitated. Nothing was visible, not trees or fenceposts or shrubs. Nothing.

I turned in the direction of our cabin and then stopped. I could not see the ground, let alone the path.

My friend sensed my confusion. "Give me your hand," she said. "I know the path well enough to get us home."

And I did.

And she did.

Looking back, I remember that occasion as a strange and meaningful journey. I trudged up the hillside, unable to see the path. Once or twice I stumbled, but her hand steadied me. There was no sound except the occasional crunch of small rocks beneath our feet. The world around us had gone to sleep, wrapped in an inky blanket.

After a few moments my uneasiness left me, and I moved with more confidence. I could not see my companion, but I held tightly to her hand. The silent minutes inched by on a soundless clock.

Then we were home.

"Take my hand," she had said. "I know the path." This is what I have remembered.

In the darkness that obscures our personal search for tomorrow, there is also One who says "Take my hand . . . I know the way."

I must not stand there, hesitating, waiting until I can see. It may be a long time until daylight, and my sight is limited. Not so, His. Additionally, He knows the path.

No, I must not stand fearfully still, but I must take His hand, and I must move forward in confidence toward the place I need to go.

He knows the way. Always.

10   "It's a Package Deal"

It's just a long strip of white paper
   Turning yellow
   But it's special
It used to be taped inside my broom closet
   Many years ago
It has tiny pencil marks, with initials and dates
   My children's initials
      And the dates I measured them
   Standing against that strip of white paper
The marks start at the bottom and go to the top
   Then there was no more room
My children outgrew the broom closet
   They stepped outside and kept growing
I need to do that from time to time
   Step outside, and keep growing.

Behold, I have set before thee an open door, and no man can shut it (Rev. 3:8, KJV).

"I'm sorry."

The salesman shook his head regretfully. "You see, we can't sell these units separately. They go together. It's a package deal."

A package deal. You can't have one without the other. Sometimes this comes in unexpected forms.

In my neighbor's home, a luxuriant green plant grew straight and tall in the corner of the small sunporch, dominating the room, projecting life and vitality. It seemed to be reaching, reaching . . .

Then it touched the ceiling. For a little while, it pushed against the solid white planks, as if its eager leaves might nudge the ceiling upward. Then, discouraged, it settled back and began to inch sideways. Finally, it stopped altogether, defeated, stunted, its vitality sapped.

It needed room to grow. And there was none.

It needed a change.

As Christians, we accept the basic premise that spiritual growth involves both Bible study and prayer. These are requisites.

Involved also is the fact that we must put into practice what we say we believe. Granted.

And then . . . ?

Then we bump our heads against the ceiling of our spiritual dwellings. We have gone as far as we can, grown as much as we can. We need to move out, to move on, if growth is to continue.

It may be time to move out of old habitats of thinking, of old ways of behaving, leaving behind the constricting ceilings which topped the rooms of yesterday. The new dwelling is much larger, with wide expanses to challenge our progress. But the road that leads upward must not be cluttered with pitfalls of past prejudices or narrowed by the range of yesterday's possibilities.

"Oh, I'd love to be there," the Christian pilgrim says, settling back in her cushioned chair and viewing a distant mountain from her comfortable backyard patio. "That is, I'd love to be there, if I didn't have to leave here!"

But you have no choice . . . if growth is to continue.

Growth involves change, sometimes external, sometimes internal.

In fact, there is no growth without change.

"It's a package deal."

11  Commas and Periods

I'm draggy before I even start
I want to avoid the whole world
I can't say I didn't sleep well
Because I did
I can't say I have a "biggie" facing me
Because I don't
I just feel "heavy" with thinking
"Heavy" with feeling
A hodge-podge of things
But today is a new day
Bright, shiny, beautiful
I need to move along
Move along, get with it
Move!

And the Lord said . . . There remaineth yet very much land to be possessed (Josh. 13:1, KJV).

"Jimmy, let me help you," the English teacher said to the restless towhead who came by after school, his latest theme drenched in red ink. "You write well. You write with feeling, with a good choice of verbs and adjectives. But you have a real problem with sentence structure, with what we sometimes call 'run-on sentences.' "

The boy eyed her with a puzzled expression.

"Let me put it this way," she went on. "There are things that belong together in one sentence, and sometimes we combine them with a comma. And that's fine, if done properly. But there are other things that should be separate. They need to stand alone. We need to end the sentence, put a period, and move along." She went on to explain the difference.

Cramming our days like our sentences with "add ons" is all too evident. We bring from our yesterdays our guilt, our tangled web of problems that settle on our consciousness and clog our thinking. Some things need to be carried forward, but all too often we allow our minds to become beasts of burden. We plod through the days with carry-overs that should have been parked earlier.

No one makes a burden lighter by continuing to carry around a load of guilt after confessing a wrongdoing, asking forgiveness, and seeking to make amends. Instead, put a period. Unload it. Move along.

No one is bettered by clinging to earlier friendships that sit like empty houses on the landscapes of our lives. If the relationship is still meaningful, we may want to infuse it with new life, or perhaps even re-structure. If not, put a period. Move along.

No one is helped by picking up the same well-nourished problem on a daily basis if the solution waits only on the decision to make a decision. Make it. Put a period. Move along.

A prominent businessman once said that a secret of his success was "Never handle the same piece of paper twice." He believed he should read the information, absorb it, and act upon it. Period.

For the Christian, this is perhaps simplistic. But the principle is valid. Sometimes, with all the input we need, we still step around the decision point and tiptoe into tomorrow, only to find the same problem there waiting for us.

The difficulty? A comma, and we need a period.

Put it down. Move along.

12 "Waiting in Action"

There's an art to waiting
  I've been told
That may be true, entirely true
  But I'm not an artist
  I can't draw at all
I guess I don't like standing still
  Like a plastic flamingo
  In someone's front yard
Just standing there, doing nothing
  Busy being plastic
  Just standing there . . .

Wait on the Lord: be of good courage, and he shall strengthen thine heart: wait, I say, on the Lord (Ps. 27:14, KJV).

"Wait on the Lord" is not a license for lethargy. On the contrary, it involves something resembling activity.

"Oh, come now," someone says. "You're not making sense. 'Waiting' and 'activity' are contradictory terms."

Not necessarily. It depends on how you wait. And it depends on your definition.

To wait is not simply to stand still. It is "to look forward expectantly."

For the Christian, waiting on the Lord begins in prayer, the prayer of faith, confident that God not only hears the petition and knows the answer, but that He will supply it.

It continues in prayer, putting aside preconceived ideas. We must not "pray the answers to our prayers" or we will block the channel.

We pray on a continuing basis because the channel which was clear yesterday may well be closed today. Impatience has slipped from the shed of self-will and tumbled into the passageway.

To wait on the Lord *does* mean to await instruction on which direction to take, but nowhere do we find the Scripture, "Thou shalt sit on thy hands while waiting."

Instead, each day we perform those tasks within our everyday reach. And interesting things begin to unfold.

It may be that while you are waiting and working, certain skills will be honed, and you will be able to open a previously closed door.

Or perhaps, as you finish the work around you, the pathway is cleared for someone to come to you, and a new avenue opens.

A third possibility exists, even a fourth.

You do the work set before you, day after day, and then suddenly you look up and the circumstances which shackled you appear quite different. "It's all changed!" you say happily. Perhaps it is. Or perhaps you have.

Or it may be that as you pray, and go about your daily ministries, you reach out just a little bit further, and move with your reach. Then one day you look up, and find yourself in a different place. Somehow, in taking care of the tasks at hand you went through an open door, and didn't even know it. In fact, looking back, you're not sure just when you went through. You just know you did.

"Wait on the Lord" is excellent advice, but it is not a license for lethargy.

In fact, it involves something that looks very much like activity.

 **Comfort**

13   Passageway

I knew, but I didn't want to know
    My friend was ill, so very ill
I didn't want to face it
    She's been family to me
    And family to my family
And I can't even begin to imagine
    A world without her in it
    Not seeing her
I cannot imagine
    Not hearing her pray
        "We are grateful to thee, our Father . . . "
I cannot imagine.

> **Peace I leave with you; My peace I give to you . . . Let not your heart be troubled, nor let it be fearful (John 14:27, NASB).**

There was something different that day.

I did not know it until I walked into her bedroom. She turned her head to greet me, and held out her hand, thin and frail from months of illness.

"I'm glad you're here," she said simply and smiled.

The room was the same, clean, airy, sunshine filtering through the blinds. The flowers lent a splash of color against the ivory walls, and the "get well" cards lined the top of the dresser. Things looked the same, yet something was different.

She watched me quietly, steadily, as though memorizing my face. And all the while, something in her eyes kept pulling at the back of my mind.

The last time I had been there, perhaps ten days previously, her eyes had been curtained as though she sought to shield some inner conflict. There had been a holding back—or was it a holding on? There had been that quiet tenacity that was so much a part of her personality.

What was different? What was I sensing?

For the first few moments, we said nothing. Words were not necessary. We had been friends for more than thirty years. Her brown eyes were clear, but increasingly I knew that something different was there.

"How was your meeting?" she asked finally.

I started to answer, but then I stumbled. What I had sensed, I now began to understand. I heard my voice replying mechanically, "Fine . . . things went well." But my mind was reeling, trying to shield itself from the bright light of discovery.

I knew what was different. In her eyes was acceptance. The tenacity, the holding on, the thrust into life was gone.

But it was not only acceptance I saw. There was peace, complete and serene.

Somehow, in the days since I had last seen her, she had fought her way through her greatest valley of shadows, and she had emerged triumphant on the other side.

"God is always more than adequate for every situation," she had said so often.

She had been through her Gethsemane. She was ready to go.

Now I must go through mine. I must let her go.

She had found Him "more than adequate." So will I. For so He is.

14 Legacy

It was an unusual story, unforgettable
About a man who didn't invest in things
    Not his money
    Not his time
He invested in people
And then an interesting thing happened
I saw the story come true
    A friend of mine died
    A friend who loved people
"She's gone," folks said, "And we'll miss her"
    Yes, we will . . . we do . . .
    But a part of her lives on
        In the people she loved.

> **Do not work for the food which perishes, but for the food which endures to eternal life (John 6:27, NASB).**

My neighbor popped in at the kitchen door. "I've brought you something," she called out.

I glanced up. Her hands were empty.

She smiled at my perplexed look.

"No, not here!" She spread out her hands. "But here!" She tapped her forehead. "Something so nice happened. I want to tell you about it.

"When your friend passed away several months ago, someone sent you a card that described a rose. It had started to climb a crumbling wall, and then, when it got toward the top, there was a crevice in the wall, and it went through, and began to bloom on the other side . . . Remember?"

I nodded.

"What I want to tell you is this: I know your friend lives on the other side, but she also lives here. Last week I went to a meeting to hear a speaker from another state. She talked about being an 'ordinary housewife,' and one day she heard a speaker emphasize what a difference one woman can make in missions. She went home saying 'What can I do in my church?' That was several years ago. Today she is the president of the women's work in that state, and sharing her enthusiasm for missions with others. I asked her later who the speaker was who had inspired her, and she told me it was your friend."

After my neighbor left, I gazed above the treetops across the street and remembered "sharings" of the past few months, coming together like a bouquet.

"I am the product of the work that your friend helped to build along the river," one had said. "And the thing I remember about her is that she cared. She cared so much for folks who had so little. And she did something about it. I'm trying to do something too."

And a secretary. "It's important around the office to do things right, not just throw them together. Real integrity goes all the way through. I learned that from her."

And an executive. "I began my professional life under her leadership. I was new, I was green, but she was an encourager. She believed in me; she believed I could do it. And I found that I could. She did that for me, and I want to do it for someone else."

And so the rose blooms . . . on both sides of the wall.

It does for her, and it does for others.

It does for all who pour themselves into the lives of their fellow human beings for Jesus' sake.

The legacy lives.

15  "Plain Vanilla Pain"

Pain and confusion
These go together
They may be the same
It all swirls around on the inside
Sometimes sharp and pointed
Sometimes vague and nebulous, free floating
There, just there
It doesn't come with an alarm clock
Or a calendar
Telling it when to move on
I guess that's up to me
To me . . . and the Lord.

But if any of you lacks wisdom, he should pray to God, who will give it to him (Jas. 1:5, GNB).

"Tell me, how do you deal with plain vanilla pain? I don't mean the biggies, like when somebody dies or a marriage falls apart. I mean the everyday ones. Your buddy throws you a curve or your girl stands you up on Saturday night. You knock yourself out studying for a final, and then the prof thinks you cheated because you made an A. It hurts. What do you do?"

It was a Sunday night university buzz session, formally called a forum. But the question the young man asked is easily paralleled in every walk of life: how do you deal with what he termed "plain vanilla pain"?

Plain vanilla may not be an accurate description. To the one hurting, no pain is plain. It comes from a complex fabric of circumstances that begins to unravel long before the loose ends are seen. And the flavor can seldom be called vanilla. It is more like "Rocky Road."

What happens first, usually?

In the confusion that surrounds pain, we all too often try to ignore the situation. Rather than dealing with it, we put it in the closet and try to shut the door. Unfortunately, we put too much of ourselves in there with it, and we keep going back.

Then we try to remedy the situation by "trying twice as hard" without ever facing the problem itself: the fact that things have changed.

Because they have, there's a hole in your life where the pain burned through. You've got to walk through it, down one side and up the other. If you try to bypass it, to play as though it never happened, you may succeed, superficially. But you'll bypass the learning that is a part of the journey, and you'll be equally vulnerable the next time around.

On your journey, consider this: Dealing with pain is not initially a matter of finding the right answers; it is first of all a matter of asking the right questions.

"Lord, I hurt, and I need your wisdom to know more about me and the way you want me to be. Where was I wrong? Is it my pride that was hurt, or me? Did I lean too hard on another human being? Did I forget that all relationships must be triangular, with You at the apex?"

"Lord, if I have been mistreated, how can I see that this does not make me less a person; how can I bypass bitterness?"

"Lord, how can I take what I have learned and help others?"

Pain is not "plain vanilla." It is "rocky road," but the path can lead upward.

16   No Small Parts

Her fingers traced the rim of the coffee cup
She talked slowly
    Hesitatingly
Trying to match words with feelings
"I have a lot of little jobs
    At the church, at the PTA
But do they really count for anything?
Maybe I'm where I need to be
It scares me to get up in front of people
    My knees get weak
    My hands get clammy
Yet there's so much to be done
And I wonder if I'm helping
    Helping at all . . . "?

Just as there are many parts to our bodies, so it is with Christ's body. We are all parts of it, and it takes every one of us to make it complete, for we each have different work to do (Rom. 12:4-5, TLB).

"I might as well be the missing person tonight, because I certainly won't be missed!"

She spoke in jest, that tall, slender grocery clerk, but there was an undercurrent of depression that belied her usually cheerful countenance.

"I won't be missed."

"I'm just one among many."

"My job really isn't that important. It's the lowest rung on the ladder."

As Christians, we are told that "The ground is level at the foot of the cross." All who hear may come to Jesus. All who hear may have equality of opportunity.

There is equality also in the Lord's work. If the ground is level, all stand on common ground, made uncommon only by individual commitment. The "level" of our service is not determined by the place we occupy on a nonexistent ladder, but rather by our openness to the task the Lord has placed before us, our willingness to be used.

Christian statesman or church custodian, executive director or part-time typist, pastor or receptionist, state president or local church worker—it's all the same. It is a job that must be done. It is a place that must be filled.

Actors sometimes say, "There are no small parts, only small actors."

Think about it.

If any one of the so-called "small parts" were not necessary, why is it there at all? It may be a "walk on" with just a few moments on stage. It may be a segment that seems unrelated or "tacked on" at the time, but the story is not finished.

Each small part is essential to the play as a whole or the playwright would not have included it in the script. It is a vital ingredient.

Without it, the play would not be complete.

Without it, the play is not an entity; it cannot make the impact it might have otherwise.

"No small parts" is true on the stage.

It is true in life also.

You *do* make a difference.

Truly, you do.

 Warning

17 The Starting Point

I like stories with happy endings
  "They rode off into the sunset . . . "
  " . . . And they lived happily ever after"
That makes for a nice feeling
  "It came out all right"
But this is just part of the picture
  Part of the story, really
A story has a beginning, a middle, and an end
  But neither the middle
    Nor the end
  Would be possible without the beginning
Beginnings are essential
  No starts . . . ?
  . . . No finishes!

He who watches the wind will not sow and he who looks at the clouds will not reap (Eccl. 11:4, NASB).

"How did your success start?" The young newsman, pencil poised over yellow pad, looked expectantly at the company president and awaited the "magic formula."

It came in unexpected form.

"If you want the truth, the real truth," the president responded slowly, "I guess it started the day I finally realized where the starting point was."

The interviewer waited.

"And that was where, sir?" he finally asked.

"Right where I was!" The older man slapped the arm of his chair. "Right here. I'm not trying to be either profound or simple—just trying to tell it like it was. There came a point in my life, a particular hour and day, when I realized that wherever it was I wanted to go, I still had to start from where I was. That had to be the starting point. Everything has to start where it is. So do people."

Everything must start from where it is.

You and I must start from where we are.

Every endeavor, be it large or small, follows the same initial format.

"But that's not always true," someone says. "I know exactly what I want to do, but I can't start until September. I'm going to college, and I won't have enough money saved until then."

Maybe we don't mean the same thing when we say "start." If you mean the point at which you and your dreams come together, and a new phase of life begins, that really isn't the starting point. By then you're already on your way. The "start" was the day you made your plans and began to save your money. You resolved to follow your dream, and you moved in that direction.

All too often by "start" we mean "begin tomorrow," some future day yet unformed by time. Then tomorrow becomes today, but our vocabulary remains unchanged. We still talk in terms of "tomorrow."

The starting point is now.

You may have a specific goal in mind; you may not. It may be a major change you feel led to make; it may be a minor matter. It may not be a "shining goal"; it may be only a beckoning path that leads beyond the crest of the next hilltop you see.

But it's there.

And you are here.

Here at the starting point.

18  Hurry, Hurry, Hurry!

Sometimes I wonder
Does all this activity make any sense?
    Hurry, hurry, hurry
Am I really accomplishing anything
Or just putting on mileage, making the rounds
    Getting back to square one
I can remember other days, less frantic
    It wasn't this way
Activities were wrapped in time
    With a little left over on the ends
Not crammed in sideways
    So that all the space was gone
What's wrong . . . ?

> **Make me know Thy ways,**
> **O Lord;**
> **Teach me Thy paths.**
> **Lead me in Thy truth and**
> **teach me**
> **(Ps. 25:4-5, NASB).**

It was a small item, boxed off in one corner of the church bulletin:

> "Three things Jesus never did:
> He never worried
> He never hurried
> He never doubted the outcome."

It was the second that caught my attention: "He never hurried."

It had been one of those hurly-burly days. That morning as I rode with a friend, I noticed she backed out of the driveway, slammed on the brakes, then gunned the accelerator to the stoplight and slammed on the brakes again. The process was repeated two more times.

Wryly I commented, as I viewed our journey and the week in retrospect, "You know, we're starting to treat ourselves the same way we treat our cars!"

All too often we do, rushing from one stop to another, and slamming on the brakes in between, as though everything were an emergency.

"But get the picture," someone says. "My life is a series of emergencies, one crisis after another."

At times, yes. But not always.

Some situations are true emergencies: the child has cut himself; the muddy waters are seeping through the cracks in the dam; the only set of car keys is lost.

Other items on our agenda are emergencies because we make them so. We fill our days so full that we rush "to get it all done." We shift out of "walk" into "run," and then after a while the gear locks.

But are most events really crises?

No, the sense of emergency usually comes not from the situations themselves, but from the fact that there are so many of them crammed into one day.

We have taken emergency patterns and made them everyday patterns. We create the monster that is our agenda, and then sacrifice ourselves to keep it going.

Certainly we should neither shirk our responsibilities nor turn a deaf ear to the friend in need. But we can plan our agendas early, led by experience rather than captured by habit.

We can learn to walk again.

And we need to.

19   People, Not Puppets

Why did I do that?
   Lashed back in anger
   Without even thinking
That's the problem
   I didn't think
   I didn't use the good sense God gave me
Someone said something I didn't like
   And I erupted
Someone flipped my switch
   And the red light buzzed
Someone pulled my string
   And I performed.

Let this mind be in you, which was also in Christ Jesus (Phil. 2:5, KJV).

The background music began, and the curtains on the darkened puppet stage opened slowly. The lights came up, bringing into view a pastoral scene with scattered trees and a wide meadow.

The music climaxed and ceased abruptly. The first puppet "strolled" onstage. With appropriate bows and flourishes, he welcomed the audience.

"This is just fantastic," a viewer on the back row whispered. "He looks just like a real person. What amazes me is that he's not doing any of it himself. Someone is pulling his strings. It's hard to realize he's a puppet, not a person."

PUPPET: A small-scale figure made to operate by an outside force.

PERSON: A human being, capable of thinking, feeling, planning, evaluating, making decisions.

At times we have to ask ourselves, "Are we people or puppets?" Do we view a situation, evaluate it, and make decisions; or are we jerked into action when someone pulls our string?

What we call action may simply be reaction. Something "spills" and we become angry, jealous, hurt. And we react.

What has happened?

We have allowed ourselves to be short-circuited. We have responded without even thinking. In other words, "Someone pulled our string" and, like puppets, we performed. Our reasoning was bypassed.

Is it wrong to respond with emotion? Certainly not. But heart and head must go together. Jesus loved deeply, but His daily ministry was consistently shaped by deliberate action.

There may be merit in using the "pause-plus" system. When something negative is suddenly dumped on us, we can pause, and then pause again. The elapsed time is only momentary, but it is deliberate. It gives us the interval we need to route what has happened through our brains—our emotions are already at work.

It gives us opportunity to think, to breathe a prayer, and to reaffirm God's presence in our lives.

It is "pause-plus."

Our responses are thus determined by our convictions, our beliefs, and not our feelings alone. We are led on by what we think, not driven on by what we feel.

We are people, not puppets.

20  In Nothing Be Anxious

Out on the edge of town
Where the highway divides
Where houses give way to cornfields
Stand rows upon rows of flat-topped mini-storage units
Hiding all manner of "things"
Behind padlocked doors
Awaiting retrieval at the proper time
Perhaps we need storage units also
For those "things" we have committed to God
"Things" that must be stored with Him
Lest our mental houses become cluttered
And anxiety overshadow our days.

> **Be anxious for nothing, but in everything by prayer and supplication with thanksgiving let your requests be made known to God (Phil. 4:6, NASB).**

"I know I shouldn't be anxious all the time, wondering how this is going to turn out . . . but I am."

Anxiety often darkens our hours, dimming the bright promise of a God-given day. We cannot enjoy the moments and the hours that make up the NOW because our thoughts rush down the road to a future responsibility or a possible problem.

Why are we this way?

Usually we are anxious because we do not know how that future "something" is going to turn out.

You may or may not be able to do anything about "something," but you can do something about YOU.

It helps to face the responsibility or the problem squarely and ask God's illumination upon the total picture. Then, considering all the possibilities as you know them, and seeking His guidance, make specific sets of plans to meet varying circumstances.

You may need to change some of your blueprints when the time comes. Rigidity makes for roadblocks; flexibility could make for different travel plans, but you will still be headed in the right direction.

Having reached your decision, breathe a prayer and deliberately commit the entire situation to the Lord. If you go over and over the same territory, you will be spinning your mental wheels on a pavement worn slick by overuse.

"I've heard that for years," you say. "I've been told many times that I must commit things to God and leave them with Him. But I don't seem to be able to do it."

It may help to visualize the importance of living in day-tight compartments, "storage units," if you will. We must do so physically; we live within that frame of time called "today." It may help to realize we can also do that mentally. We can visualize each day as a special segment or compartment. We live within that day.

Today, we can dream for tomorrow. Indeed, we must. And we need to make plans. But we also need to recognize such activities for what they are: mental work done today to be stored in one of tomorrow's compartments and implemented at some future date. Not today.

You need not be anxious because "I don't know." Yours is a finite mind. You cannot know the infinite. Only God can.

But you have done your part and stored it with God. Now enjoy today.

Sharing

21   Cart Before the Horse

I'm not sure what went wrong
    But something did
We worked so hard to go over the top
    But we missed it
Sometimes I feel that way in my Christian life
    Not always, but sometimes
I volunteer to get something done
    I work hard
    And then it doesn't jell
Something must be wrong somewhere
    Backwards, maybe?

Love the Lord your God with all your heart, soul, and mind . . . Love your neighbor as much as you love yourself (Matt. 22:37, 39, TLB).

"Don't get the cart before the horse" was an admonition that made sense in Grandma's day.

It may be a little hard for her grandchildren to visualize "how it was" through eyes that see today's world of jet planes and spaceships, yet the truth remains. Today we are no different in one basic aspect: our world is made up of people. Many people. And our world has needs. Many needs. But a host of people can meet a heap of needs . . . if they work together. It's called teamwork.

All too often we focus on the finish line instead of the

starting point—loving people, building relationships. We plunge forward and muddle through, heading in approximately the same direction but with divided efforts. Results are disappointing.

What went wrong? The cart may have been in front of the horse. Our goal may have been a worthy one, but the team power was unharnessed. Love had not shown itself strongly enough to build relationships.

"I keep coming back to this," the seminar leader said to a gathering of executives. "Remember the strong connection between relationships and results. Forget it at your peril."

It is true in the marketplace.

It is true in the Christian realm.

It is true horizontally and vertically as we relate to each other and to God.

For best results in the human arena, we concentrate first on teamwork. We must have not only a shared vision and a common commitment, but we must also respond to people as individuals. We must develop a togetherness of spirit before we can move forward in a productive way. Relationship is the harness that binds us all together, but it must be created, brought into being.

Then the results will be different. Success cannot be guaranteed, but the possibility is strengthened.

The importance of relationship works vertically also.

We must be committed to God's world plan—missions—sharing His word.

We must be committed to our individual part in that plan. "Serving God," we call it.

But no service for Him can take the place of devotion to Him.

Service is not a substitute for relationship; service results from relationship.

Let's not get the cart before the horse.

Pass it on.

22   A Glimpse of Tomorrow

So many times we have been told
"Children have more need of models than critics"
    And that's true
    But does it go far enough
    Just having someone "to look up to"?
      It may be too loose a link
Don't we need to do more
    Move closer, perhaps
      Be near
      Communicate
      Touch . . .

"Simon . . . do you really love me?"
"Yes, Lord," Peter said, "you know I am your friend."
"Then take care of my sheep," Jesus said (John 21:16, TLB).

She was small and red-headed, and not particularly pretty. But there are many who remember her influence as being a dominant factor in their college lives.

An English professor in a small state school, she invested hours in continuing preparation for her classes, but she invested even more in her students.

She was surprised when someone asked her about her "effective methods" of working with young people. "I guess I see them first as they are, and then as they can be," she replied.

"Do you remember the story of Michelangelo?" she asked. "One time he supposedly sat and stared at a block of marble, and finally someone asked him what was so interesting about that particular block. He explained that he didn't see the block at all—he saw the angel inside.

"Well, I change that a little. I need to see them first as they are. I meet with them individually and get to know them. There are some similarities, yes, but each one is an individual. I come to know their talents, their strengths, their weaknesses. And I begin to see what each one could be and share that vision with them.

"It would not be right for me to impose my thinking on them. Not at all. Certainly I could not structure their futures and expect them to fit into it. I am not wise enough, nor am I willing to do so. But rather, I want to help them see what they can be, to catch the vision; and, if they do grasp it, then we can share it. We can work together to make it come true."

She took time to know them individually.

She took time to share with them a vision of what they could be.

She took time to stay in touch, to reaffirm by a little visit, a pat on the shoulder. Or, when graduation had stretched the miles between them, she wrote little notes. The content was different, but the message was the same: "I care about you."

She took time.

In reality, time was not taken; it was invested. And that investment has paid uncounted dividends. Many rise up to call her blessed: a professor who teaches very much as she did, a corporation executive, a missionary, a college registrar.

"I see them first as they are, and then as they can be . . . It's like a glimpse of tomorrow."

Pass it on.

23  "Come . . . and Go"

Those faraway places . . . dim, distant, exotic
  Call to my nomad spirit
And I find myself musing
  "Wouldn't it be wonderful
  To work in Rio, or Nairobi, or Hong Kong
  I could do great things . . . Surely!"
But then I think of Jesus
  In Jerusalem, in Cana
He wasn't in distant places
  Never far from home
And I remember the neighbor across the street
  And a family down by the tracks
I wonder . . . chances are
  This is my Jerusalem . . . for now.

Freely you received, freely give. (Matt. 10:8, NASB).

The young pastor paused at the conclusion of his sermon, his gray eyes sweeping the congregation. "Carry this thought with you," he said, emphasizing each word, "The same Lord who said 'Come' also said 'Go.' "

And Jesus did.

A strong relationship exists between "come" and "go."

We use the words individually, but more often than not we pair them together, albeit subconsciously. The friend who comes to see you will probably be leaving . . . going. The rain that comes will be stopping . . . going.

"If winter comes, can spring be far behind?" is poetic philosophy; but it says that winter will be coming, and it will also be going.

"Come on, it's time to go" speaks of an even closer connection.

Why, then, in our Christian life, do we tend to separate "come" and "go"? Why do we seem to believe that our responsibility is just to come to the Lord?

Is it not true that a gift is given to be used, be it utilitarian or ornamental? If it is utilitarian, it may even have an instruction sheet, telling us what to do. If we read the instruction sheet, we may appropriate the full value of the gift—use it to the maximum. If not, we may not be able to realize the gift's full potential.

In all areas of life, our "instruction sheet" is the Bible. And it instructs us to "Go and tell."

You may be called to Kenya . . . or Peru . . . or Spain . . . or Taiwan. Perhaps.

You may be called to Atlanta . . . or Chicago . . . or New Orleans . . . or New Mexico. Perhaps.

You may be called to work in your home area. And not perhaps. But assuredly. Without doubt.

Why don't we follow instructions?

Perhaps we forget that a gift (in this case, the gift of salvation) is given to be used.

Perhaps we forget that "come" and "go" are bound together. We don't want to be like the vessel that comes to be filled, and then, having been filled, sits there until the contents are dried up or evaporated. Rather, we want to share what we have received, pour it out, and, like the cruze of oil or the loaves and fishes, see it multiplied.

The gospel came to us on its way to someone else . . . hopefully.

Don't break the chain.

Pass it on.

24 The Candle

On center stage, alone
One girl held high a single candle
    A soft, steady glow
    In the circular vastness of the dark coliseum
She stood motionless
    Then moved to one side, then the other
    Lighting one candle here, a second there
Up the rows, across the rows, the light traveled
    Four . . . eight . . . sixteen
And soon the giant coliseum glowed with a thousand candles
The darkness was gone
    Because one candle was lit
    One light was carried
    One light was shared.

Eternal life is in him, and this life gives light to all mankind. His life is the light that shines through the darkness—and the darkness can never extinguish it (John 1:4-5, TLB).

It happened many years ago near a small town that hugged the edge of the mountain. The night was dark and moonless. In the tiny railroad station that sat where the tracks began to curve around the mountain, the only noise was the clack of the telegraph as the late night messages crackled over the wire.

The operator, leaning back in his chair, suddenly bolted upright, a look of horror washing over his face as the message rattled on. The train that passed earlier had lumbered to a stop just beyond the curve, out of sight from the station. The reason was not clear, but it was there. And another train, not scheduled to stop at his station, was due to roar past on the same track in a matter of minutes.

He leaped to his feet, grabbed the kerosene lantern, and rushed out into the night. In the distance he saw the oncoming train. Standing as close as he dared to the tracks, he began to signal.

The train rushed toward him, its speed unslackened. Frantically now, he waved the lantern in a wide arc, but the train thundered past and rounded the curve. In a few minutes he heard the frenzied whistle, the screech of the brakes, and the splintering crash.

Sickened in mind and body, he looked down in despair, and his eyes fell on the lantern.

It was unlit.

Without the light, its message had been swallowed up in the blackness of the night. All of his activity had been in vain.

The Christian has a problem that is similar, yet different. The divine light is there, ready to guide, to empower. But it is not always used.

What we say we do "for Him" may involve astute planning and unremitting effort. It may impress our co-workers and dazzle the sideliners with our abilities and energies. But if it is self-propelled, it will count for little on the eternal yardstick.

It is what we truly do for Him, impelled by inner light rather than outer appearance, that makes the difference.

The candle is lit, ready for use.

The choice is yours.

Pass it on.